MW00626494

sage
soul
and
flowers

Sage Soul and Flowers

ISBN: 978-1-7367817-0-8

Artist: Brooke Kelley
Editor: Colleen Nufer

Dedication

This book is dedicated to all my friends and family who shower me with love and encouragement, and to all those who dare to feel, to create, and to just simply be.

Sage Soul and Flowers
Sage is the wisdom that I crave.
Soul is the essence of who I am and the beauty I see in you.
Flowers are my joy, my teacher, and my inspiration.
I hope my poetry makes you think, dream, believe, and love.
Jen Adams

Sweet Like a Cherry

Love roams freely in the field,
Its beat beautifies and heals,
It rides on the back of the spotted hued horse,
It beats so boldly,
It knocks down doors,
But that love seldom dares to enter.
This love is on fire and decorates each room with its embers,
It's sweet like a red cherry,
And magical as the garden fairy.
It blows in the wind, riding next to the butterflies,
It touches and pierces all who are standing by.
This love is a miracle and cherished by many,
It surrounds the sunsets, coloring the land with plenty.
Warm and soft, it wraps around you,
It sees your gifts, maybe some you never even knew.
A love more precious than the shiny stone,
Its energy unites and rests in your bones.
Love that makes you hungry for more,
Love that you cherish,
Love that you adore.
And who is the one behind the beat,
Who is the one this love creates?
The wonder of waves,
Ceasing to stop their ways.
The red, the round, the love that has been found.
It seeps, and it spills,
Holes of fears and doubts it fills.
It shines, and it spreads,
And does it again.
A love like a giant sequoia tree,
It grows wild and free,
For all to see.
For all to have, for all to be.

What Really Matters

This life, it could all be so easy.
We could live together happily,
If I believe in you and you believe in me.
Why do we feel the need to prove that we're right?
Could we allow some space for others and not put up a fight?
To take a pause,
Not react to every cause.

Could you have the sight to see who I am,
To stop for a minute and understand my plan?
Not to tell me what you think I should be,
But allow me to create the life that makes me happy.

Could you have the courage to let others fail?
To let them feel whatever arises,
Not rushing to seek their bail,
To sit in discomfort and know that it will pass.
It might take a while or peace might come fast.
To know the noble truth that suffering exists,
And to realize that detachment offers pure bliss.
Being open to everything, with a heart full of joy,
To notice the spirit in each girl and boy.

What if we lived from a place of true love?
Competition and self-centeredness carried away
On the wings of the dove.
If we understood that we all want the same things,
It's not about the stuff and fancy rings.
Nothing can wipe the tears from your eye,
Or hug you and love you so much you could cry.

Yet, we find ourselves chasing things that don't matter,
Overlooking the heart of our brothers and sisters.
Imagine a world where we all really care,
Where empathy trumps winning or becoming a billionaire.

Be the Life

Be the tree,
And the bird flying free.
Be the blue ocean,
Synchronized motion.
Be the painted sky,
The sunset and sunrise.
Be the bold mountains,
And the awareness of your emotions.
Be the life,
Living through you.
Be the daring dancer
And your own
Guru.

Can the Fish See the Ocean

Can the fish see the ocean,
Can the bird see the sky
Can an eye see an eye,
Questions fly by,

Do these questions have wings,
Can the moon hold a swing,
Is there hope in a wedding ring,
Do you feel the ground under your feet,
Or do you hurry along
Tasks to complete?

Can you see the air that you breathe,
Can you remember your time in the womb,
Can you hear the silence in a room,
Does a cow know he moos,
Does a cat know she meows,
Does a rooster know he crows,
Does a lion know she growls,
Does a baby hear its cries,
Does a dog understand goodbyes,
Can you feel a heartbeat from across the room,
Do you understand the science of a sonic boom,
Can you see connection,
Can you touch rejection, or maybe perfection,
Can you hear heaven above,
Can you see the peace that clothes the dove,
Can you feel the roots growing under the tree,
Do you see the magic planted in every seed,
Can you see the wind chilling your skin,
Can you know the peace within,
Can you hear the stars twinkling in the night sky,

Or our ancestor's words where their tribes passed by,
Can you hear what's not said,
Grab a hold of the thoughts in your head?

Can you smell a smile or juggle joy,
Can you feel a fear,
See the sounds entering your ear,
Does a bird know it flies,
Does it see the clouds pass by,
Does a worm see the dirt,
Does it have feelings to hurt,
Does a branch know its trunk,
Can the earth feel the trash and the junk
Can you know what's true,
By looking inside you?

Can you know with your body and not just your head,
Can you allow some contrast without fear and dread,
Can you taste the perfection in the food from the ground,
Can you share your lessons,
Each one that you've found,
Can you touch your desires,
Feel them burn like a fire,
Can you know who needs help
Before the asking arrives,
Can you see the struggle when looking in their eyes,
Can you taste the joy as the sun greets the sky,
Can you share your love with all who pass by?

Can you grasp a different story,
One that sets you free,
Can you see your mind move and change your beliefs,
Can you feel the courage to allow it to be,
Can you imagine your dreams,
Can you hold onto to hope,
Can you flip frustration into a joke?

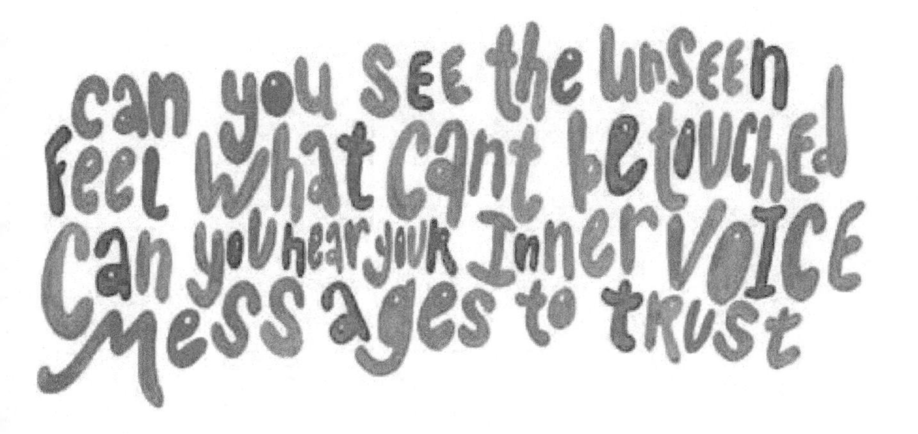

To Be Found

Life can be so big sometimes,
We spin and turn and need to unwind.
To find a space that's calm and bright,
To sleep peacefully throughout the night.
To be found and seen
On someone to lean.
To know you matter,
And that someone cares.
To have a purpose
And the courage to dare.
To live your life from an honest spot,
No worry or fear of what you're not,
Or what they might say
Or even do,
But to be found in yourself
And others too.

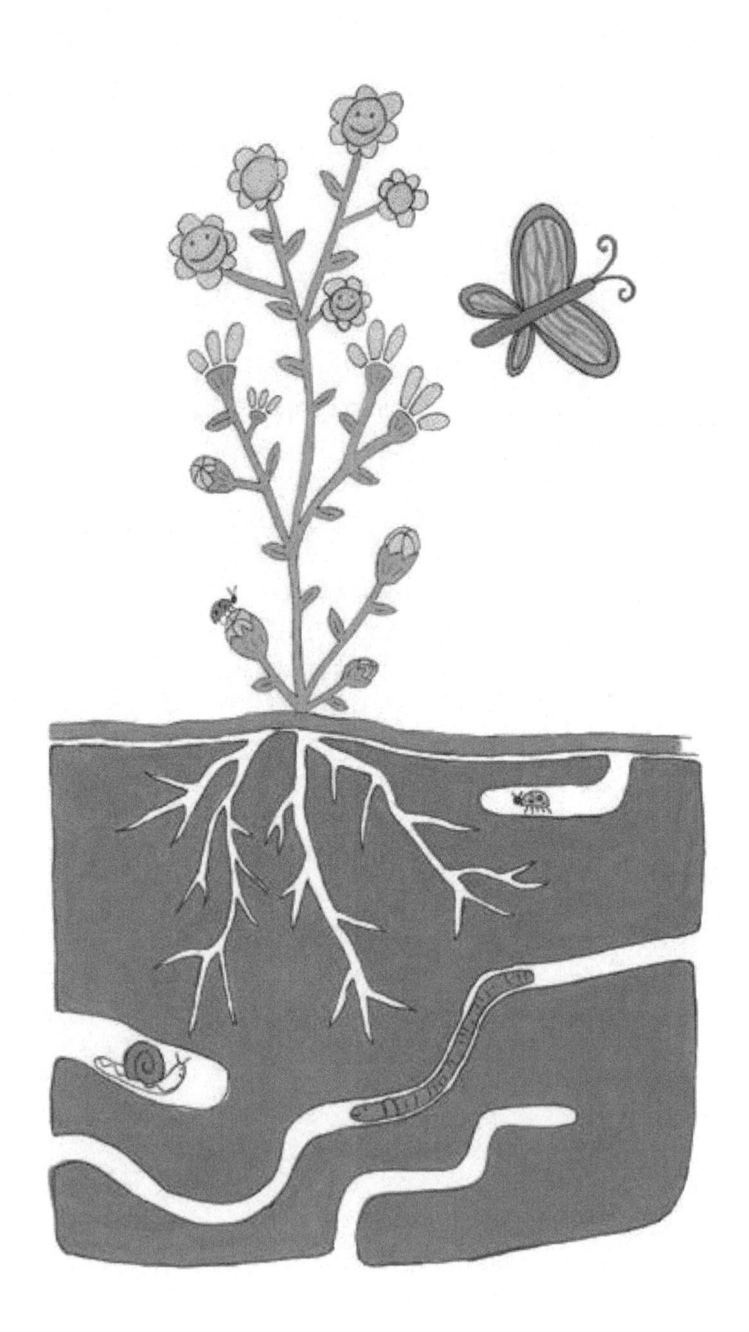

The Waiting Game

The waiting game is real.
The longing, the wanting,
One cannot steal.
Waiting it must be.
If it's peace, if it's love, or if it's money,
Needn't worry,
Waiting it must be.
For if we grasp and hold too tight,
What we want will put up a fight.
Let it be,
Cast our worries out to sea.
For what we desire will rear its head,
Our dreams and desires are not dead.
Listen and be ready,
We will be led.
Like the flower waiting to bloom,
Petals blossoming in warm sun rays,
Roots spreading and finding new waterways.
But it hurts, you say,
My heart aches every day.
My eyes keenly see the void inside of me.
My shoulders slump, my head hangs low.
I want to be content, complete;
I want to glow.
Patience, what's that?
I want what I want,
Just like that.
But let this all go,
I feel the fire,
I feel the fear,
Focus on the moment, the view will become clear.
Life,
A masterpiece painting,
Colors all worth the waiting.
Be present and breathe,
Let each moment form as it should be.

Rainbows

Rainbows and ribbons,
Pigtails and cocktails,
Morphing into me.
Face in the mirror,
Who I dare to be.
Should I, shades the day.
Colors of the rainbow,
Brighten the way.

All of me for you today.
We glow in the prism of the waterway.
A pot of gold,
Or so they say.
Colors of a rainbow,
For this I pray.
And when it fades,
Fades softly away
I go about my beautiful day.

What Are You Searching For?

What are you searching for
The perfect life
A handsome man or a beautiful wife
A life free of strife
Rainbows and ice cream sundaes
Big winds that send the clouds away
Feeling good, free from pain.
No heartaches, only joy to gain
A big house and a fancy car to drive
Is this what makes you feel alive
New shoes and a shiny ring
How much peace do they really bring
Maybe peace is not the goal
Material things and not looking old

When you close your eyes,
Can you imagine the perfect life
Will you like who you are on the day you die
What do you chase
Does it bring a smile to your face
Do others enjoy your space
How do your ways affect your days
If you asked,
What would others say
Do you care
Or is the chase a challenge, a dare
Are you searching for the meaning of it all
The answers to the colors in the fall
Why the good die young
Why religion and politics result in a brawl
Do you run towards the light
Or stagger and crawl
Numbered are the days
Seek and you shall find,
How is your life designed?
Be the sculptor of your mantel piece,
Dust it off and shine the light
It represents a beautiful life
Take a minute
Maybe, right now
Ask what it is you're searching for
Meditate, even if you don't know how
Close your eyes, relax your brow
Look inside
And when you're done
Take a deep breath
And bow

I Can't Make You See

I can't make you see
What I know you can be
I can't make you believe
The gifts inside of you
They're planted and sprouted
Waiting to be watered by you
Let the sunshine in
Through the holes in your skin
Where the fears and the faults have left their marks
The light will heal and your future will be revealed
Rain from the sky
Feed the seeds on the inside
Follow the stars
Like Joseph from long ago
Nature speaks and you will know

To Pause...

To respond mindfully, not reacting
To enjoy the wake of each day
And patiently wait
The unveiling of the mysteries
To touch freedom and taste peace
Before I rest my eyes
To flow through the moments
Regardless of the circumstances
To wear the coat of love
And burn the cape of fear, and erase negative thoughts
To be washed away by the mid-winter rain
To know my truth, forget trying to prove
To be bold and authentic
Regardless of the audience
To embrace empathy
To lead with compassion
Holding it tight
Softly expressing it
Readily giving it away
To smile and laugh along the way
To eat and dance
To paint and pray
To serve and listen
And to hear my calling
To be aware of the details
And clearly focused on the big picture
To know my body is an anchor
And acknowledge that I am a spiritual being
To honor my breath
And eat the food that serves my body
To let nature bathe me, inspire me, and teach me
To connect me with what is beyond this world
To follow the colors of the rainbow
Towards the path that was paved for me
To use my gifts and passions to touch the lives of others

To seek to listen
To be ready to receive
To stay in a good vibration
To notice the spaces between the spaces
The sounds between the sounds
To know the truth, deep in my soul
To live from the inside out
To do with less and try my best
To release with each exhale and believe with each inhale
To be aligned with the source
Writing poems that rhyme
To know everything will be fine
To inspire and teach, to go beyond my reach
To make someone feel loved or noticed
For even just one moment
To show some care to those who breathe some painful air
To laugh a lot
Especially at myself
To smile a bunch and listen to the hunch
To look beyond what's in plain sight
To know what's real, what's raw, what's right
To step all over fear, or simply walk away
To know I'm safe from what others might say
To get over the bad
Think thoughts that don't make me feel sad
To be consistent
Refuse resistance
To dispel awkward moments that don't mesh
To strive to be my best
To see the beauty in the smallest change
To believe it will come
Everything
We are one
To rest at night and dream upon the clouds, soft and white
To fulfill my soul
My journey to be told

KIND
NESS

Stuffed With Love

Everyone is trying to figure it out
Today and tomorrow
Fear and doubt
Some are calm and simply carry on
Others fret, don't follow where led
What inspires you to make a change
To free yourself, break through the chains
Days pass by and turn into years
Nothing is different, the path is unclear
A boy passes by, with a look in his eye
He knows what he wants
Words written in bold fonts
He makes his plan as he starts each day
He looks inside, he dreams and prays
Each step he takes turns over a rock
Joy and gratitude, he feels a lot
He watches his dreams build before his eyes
His passion and love keep him alive
Others notice something, different indeed
He has no possessions, he aims to please
To make his life one of ease
To spread kindness is what he does
There's plenty inside
He's stuffed with love

Passionate Life

Wanting it all and more than that,
Loving life, and funky hats.
Seeing the world and sharing a laugh,
Sitting on the sand with pen in hand.
Creativity and expression, ideas, and inventions.
Plump with passion,
Make it all happen.
Slow the moments,
Give me more time,
So I can do, be, and find.

A whimsical garden,
Fruit on every vine,
Colors so bright,
Visible to even the blind.
Music plays,
And dancing breaks out,
People are in love,
And there is no doubt.
The world swirls in the fluffy clouds above,
Sharing and giving,
So much love.

Gypsy Soul

Gypsy soul
Mystic flow
All things new and old
The river flows
Feel the blood go
Boats in the water and we row
Downstream we sail
All victory, no fail
Stories told
Mysteries unfold
Doors open and close
Answers she knows
River ends
At the grassy bend
Gypsy soul
Mystery flow!

Writing

So, what if I wrote another poem tonight,
Would I come up with words that might offer delight.
Should I just go to bed and call it a night.
So many moons have I stayed up to see,
So many stars that looked down upon me.
There's a freedom in the night, all sleeping peacefully.
The quiet intrigues and energizes me.
I stay awake and ponder eternity.
I revel in the expansion of creativity.
Living a lifestyle of flexibility.
A freedom is carried on the scent of the night bloom,
It sneaks through the window and enters my room.
Senses ignite, writing words gives me delight.

Creations on paper, a gift to my soul,
Now I extend sharing stories both new and old.
Feelings and thoughts and lessons on my path,
A new love and desire to broaden my craft.

and so it
goes

And So It Goes

Mountains form, babies are born.
War, we have it.
Peace, we want it.
Hearts break, it's hard to escape.
Love prevails, it never fails.
Bumps and bruises we get,
The hug or kiss you never forget.
Fall in the mud, shoes get wet.
When gratitude shines, there is no debt.
Earth shakes, floods abound, compassion is organically found.
Sun relentless with its rise,
A star's twinkle that never dies.
Crashing waves upon the sloped shore,
The curiosity of God's lore.
Blood rushing through my veins,
It's only I who can take the reins.
Happens as it does,
As my skin sags and the days eat my youth.
As I worry or cry,
And contemplate what happens when I die.
As I buzz with glee,
The sky says, let it all be.
It is what it is,
My mind sets me free.

Mirror

What you see in me is what I see in you
Polarity
All you want
You already have
I'm simply reflecting your essence
Do grab
Your loving spirit
That fills the room
The positive energy traveling to the moon
Around it goes and back again
To land upon your lovely skin
Close your eyes and turn inside
You don't have to travel far and wide
Your answers are found right here on the ground
Messages have been sent from forces above
Tune into yourself and know you are love

The Life of a Flower

The flower sleeps beneath
It's dark and wet, yet she sees the light
She spreads her arms and legs
Pushing through the dampness
Reaching for new lands
Finally, she is gifted with the light
She feels the warmth on her body and the wind blows her unstable
Singing to the sun, she begins to grow strong
Her petals expand and her colors develop quickly,
Like a blush of embarrassment

The flower feels the same
Yet different.
One day she breathed the midafternoon delight
A small hand held her tight
She felt a tug and life began to escape with the passing breeze
Yet, as she is held and smelled
She knows no condition to her love.
And suddenly
She feels free
Reborn in the grip of a hand
Awakened
For eternity

Last Days

Nobody knows when the day will come.
How many more sunrises will sneak through the cracks.
And, if we knew, what would change,
Who would we share our time with,
What would we rearrange.
What would we do to serve or bring us pleasure,
Would life be about meaning or fun or neither.
Judgement would surely melt away.
The beauty of all things would rise to the top,
The separation of oil and water,
Blame, we would surely drop.
Questions may dance around in your head,
Or maybe peace across your body would spread.

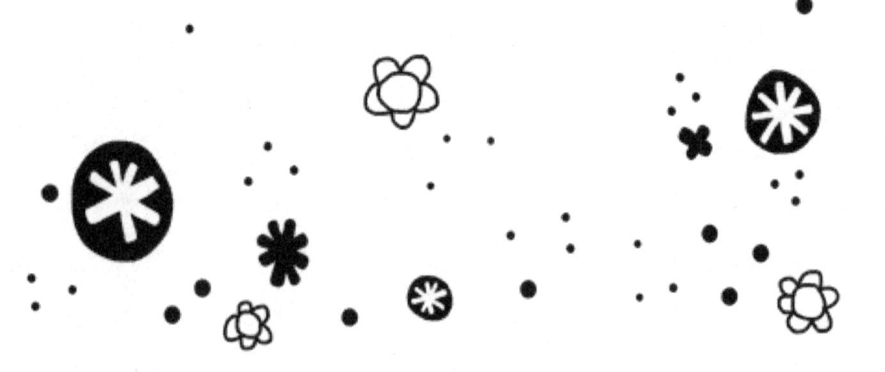

And is it possible to live in this way,
To treat this one as it might be your last day?
To walk with a mind so clear of distractions,
To notice the joys and nature's perfections.

To live from your truth,
Open from the core,
To be present as you walk out the door.

To crumble our walls and fall into empathy,
To embrace and smile at those around me.

So in this way, I'd like to stay,
With this feeling in my heart, with gratitude in my cart.

For I know not when my days will end.
I wish to spend them with my friends,
To be a light and sure of my plight.
To matter in some way, each and every day.

Can You See Your Soul

Can you know the value of love
Without the threat of it being gone
Can you feel the hope in the coming of dawn
Can you breathe so deep and accept YOU down to the core
Do waves understand why they reach for the shore
Can you see inside your soul, do you know it exists
Can you feel the seasons as they begin to shift
Does a salmon know that she's swimming upstream
Does the universe really know everything
If reality had pigment, what color would it be
What if hate had a price and peace was truly free
Does God know my voice
Does nature have a choice
Do you know when you blink, does pain make you think
Can you swallow satisfaction, and pour joy into your drink
Can you hear the mystery in the falling white snow
Can you see the miracle as the seeds begin to grow
Can you feel the artist from the painting on the wall
Do the colors touch you, can you hear the call
Can you hear the music as the trees answer to the wind
Do you know the subtle messages within
Can you feel the relief as the sun flattens on the horizon
As the colors morph from yellow, orange and green
Do you feel blessed in this magnificent scene
And, again, when it awakes,
Can you feel the hope as the day breaks
Can you feel the imagination as the sun greets the sky
As clouds softly drift on by
Can you see that all is really possible
Can you believe that
You are a
Miracle

    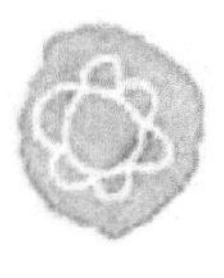 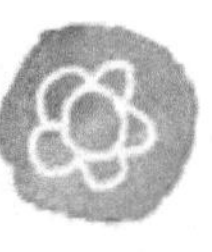 

Can you smell the darkness when it comes
Do you feel the urge to pick up and run
Can you feel every emotion, not shunning, nor running
Can you know that love is the only magic potion
Can you embrace all that you are
Aging and evolving from near to far
Can you taste all that life gives you
Can you breathe it in and become renewed
Can you hug and love along the way
Can you align yourself with empathy each day
Can your skin ooze forgiveness
Can your soul know it's right
Can you see and greet gratitude each and every night
Do angels really sing
Does chanting change anything
Can you reach for the moon
And believe your wishes will come soon
Can you open your heart and know your part
Can you hear the silence between the notes
Do you know the punchline behind the jokes
Can you sense the loneliness in those around
Can you extend a hand, say something profound
Can you lose the fight, of trying to be right
Can you allow life to flow, to expand. and grow
Can you loosen the grip and just enjoy the trip
Can you let me be me, no judgement to see
Connected we are,
Connected for eternity.

What is Real?

Is it the stains on my skin,
Or the jeans I try to fit in.
Is it the flower,
Or the garden on the hill.
Is it the frustration,
And stress that I feel.
What is real?
A dream at night,
The things within my sight.
Is it something I can touch,
My senses brushed.
The eyes through
Which I see.
Things begin to twirl.
All that surrounds the outside of me,
Everchanging, impermanent you see.
What is real?
It can only be,
That which resides inside of me.
Only what I truly believe,
We're all created perfectly.
A soul reaching to burst,
Out of space,
Freely expanding,
Dancing in grace.

No Veil

Wake me up to something bigger
With the light of awareness
Shining upon me.
As the afternoon sun soothes me
May my mind be at peace,
May my veil be removed,
As I stare straight into the light,
No squinting affecting my sight.
Open and brave,
Not just for today.
Walk through life
With a courageous stride
Not intoxicated by fears.
Lift the veil, my dear.

Beautiful Beach

Footprints and sea glass,
Tiny rocks and birds that pass.
Gentle sounds and rolling waves,
Make the landscape my view today.
Logs tossed ashore and shells to adore,
Sunshine making diamonds on the surface allures.
People stroll by with heads at a bow,
Looking for treasures and peace, somehow.
Perhaps it is found on the beautiful beach,
While taking it in,
With sandy feet.

Believing Our Test

Ideas swirling around like the wind.
Waiting for the calm and clarity to step in.
So many thoughts tossing around in my head.
Looking for guidance and the road to be led.
Peace and harmony looming around the corner,
Make moments count,
Life is a loaner.
Believe in yourself and your body will follow.
Actions and behaviors behind thought will grow.
Assume you're the best while minding the rest.
Perfection, our gift.
Believing, our test.

We Are One

Together under the giant sun.
A path, muddy and dark.
Reaching for the stars, the brightness where we once start.
A windy path, potholes, and roadblocks.
Blurred sight, blinded by fright.
Pain, a dagger in the chest.
Confusion, anxiety, no rest.
Question marks paint the walls.
A ladder, a cane, no help, we fall.
A stretched-out arm, a loving voice, a school yard for a new choice.
Together under the giant sun, communion, empathy,
Towards love we run.
Where the road leads, we don't know.
Trust and peace will show.
Together we surround the sun, hands held, hearts beating as one.
Beating for love of our daughters and sons.
We are one.

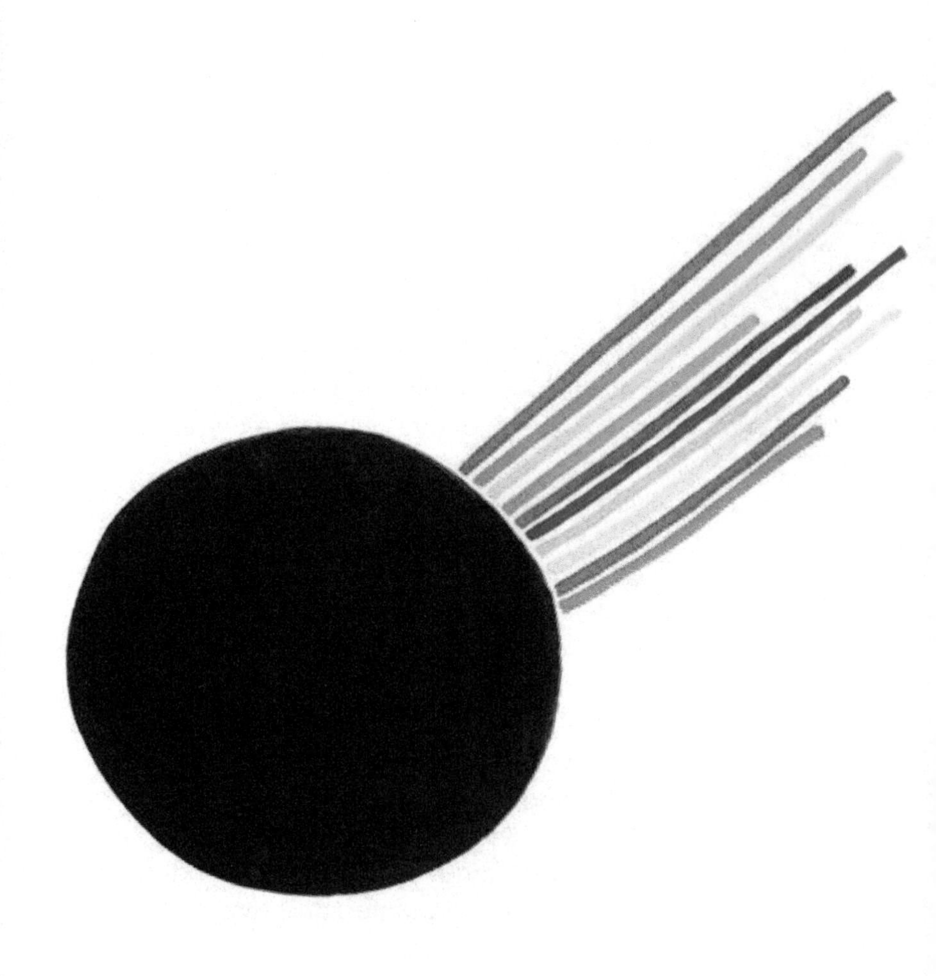

Moments in Time

Another dimension of space and time,
Perhaps.
Powerful experiences,
That last.
Time stops,
But travels fast.
Focus and feeling,
Energy around the body wraps.
All else fades away,
Blurry watercolor on canvas,
They stay.
These moments,
Moments to crave,
Awareness invades.
Warm flames from the fire by night,
Sitting in peacefulness,
Connecting in the light.

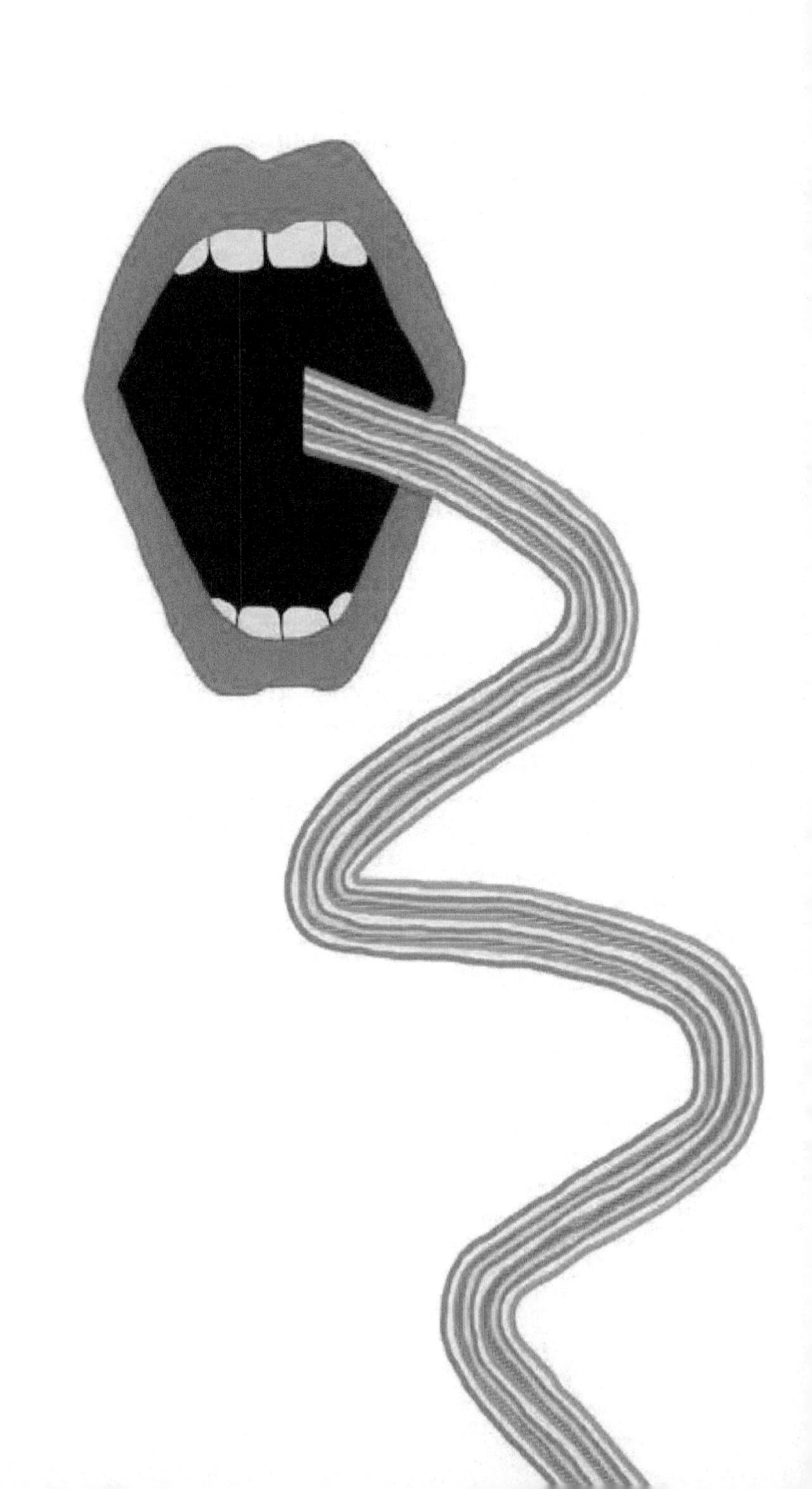

Impermanence

I'm only renting these feet of mine,
They carry the weight of my body just fine.
These legs, they take me to the shore each day,
They move me and groove me and allow me to play.
I'm only renting these arms of mine,
They extend to the world, give and receive so fine.
I'm only renting these eyes,
I see the spirit in you, so sweet.
I see the pain and the secrets you keep.
I'm only renting this mouth of mine,
I teach and I talk, connecting in time.
I'm only renting this belly of mine,
My honest guide that keeps me in line.

Peace Knows Where to Find Me

The dreamer dreams
Living in a fantasy
A dream
In a world
Safe
A space that is
Free
Vibrant
Warm breezes
Blow
Scents of trees
Awaken spirits
Peace
Knows
Where to find
Me

EXCUSE US, WE'RE GOING THIS WAY

On the Path

On the path,
What does this mean,
Follow the straight and narrow?
That path sounds boring.
Wide open with lots of turns and curves,
Now, that sounds exciting,
Like an adventure worth forging.
Are we afraid of the turns,
What might come up, what feelings might churn.
What we might encounter and actually like,
Contrary to what we've been told since a little tyke.
To walk the curved path,
Takes courage and an attitude that will last.
For in the crevices and turns so sharp,
You might find some discoveries that pierce your heart.
Are you brave enough to continue the walk,
To take the steps, feelings unlocked.
To know that the rough parts will eventually become smooth.
To be authentic and fearless as you put on your shoes.
To have fun, faith, and trust in this path,
Enough to smell the flowers as you move past.
Which journey will you take,
One that reveals, or one that is fake?

Mysterious Life

Winding, turning, falling, and rising.
Forming, building, lasting, and trusting.
Growing, changing, staying, and leaving.
Flying, gliding, climbing, and sliding.
Knowing, questioning, feeling, and thinking.
Laughing, smiling, crying, and grimacing.
Discovering adventures, out of bounds and wild.
Cultures, languages, food, and music.
Babies and grandmas.
Birth and death.
Love and heartache, contentment, and longing.
Winds of mystery, moons of wonder.

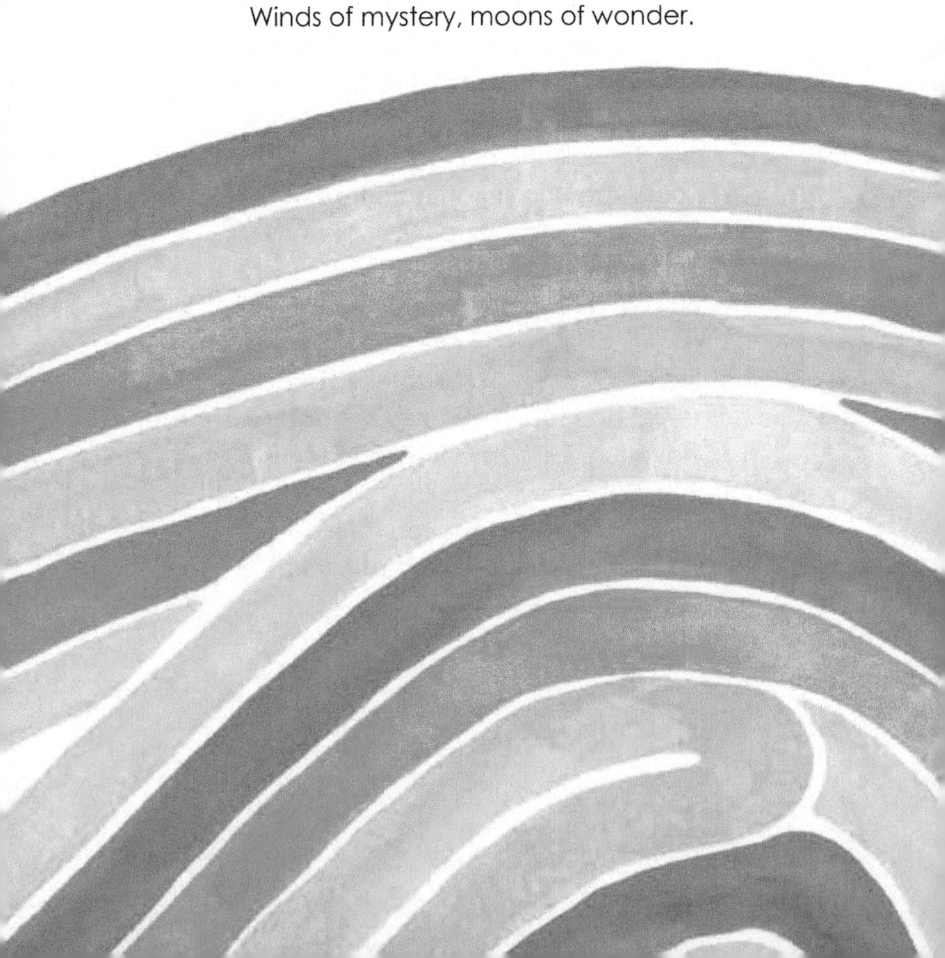

Sun of joy and mountains of endurance.
Oceans of power and flowers of fragrance.
Creatures of curiosity and trees of peace.
Earth and re-birth, place our feet upon its dirt.
Stand tall and firm,
Look beyond the rivers and the berms.

LET it
go and
LET IT
FLOW

It's Time

It's time to have some fun.
Time for creation.
It's time to enjoy the sun's rotation.
No more standing still,
Stagnation be gone!
It's time to loosen the grip.
It's time to take a long trip.
It's time for allowing, even just a bit.
Gone are the dark days.
Vines of light and love spilling over time.
It's time,
This time is mine.
I share it with you now,
Excitement with a raised brow.
Time wrapped with a bow,
Let it go and let it flow.

Dreaming Awake

Living in a dream
Reality stained with wanting
Yet inspired by the notion
Soul played like an old guitar
Strumming and tapping
Music heard from afar
Dreaming awake
This isn't fake
Curious about fate
Natural and deep
Emotions seep

Life is a gift
Not wanting to miss
Anything
Especially this
Vulnerability
More to say
Vulnerability stays away
Feelings known
Can't get it out
Wanting to shout
Heart pounds, eyes well up
Being known
Fills my cup
Courage caress me
Layers, fall away freely
Carve a new path
Make it easy to pass
Line the road
With bright flowers
For my stories to be told
For my feelings to grow bold

Change

Everything comes to an end.
A camp of natives gathering, now a bed of grass.
Equally as beautiful, but not the same.
And nothing ever is,
The same.
Want we might, to force it is trite,
Molecules moving at the speed of light.
Trees grow tall, branches brown and fall.
Flowers bloom and turn to seed.

I shrink, I swell,
Always changing every tiny cell.
If only I could hold some things so tight.
A grip on the joys that I love in my life.
If I could wave my lavender wand on all the stories I find so fond,
If I could thrive in a magical place where change only exists,
Even with the darkness that wants to persist.
I'd skip and I'd jump,
Throw my hands in the air.
I promise to be grateful and treat this gift with care.

If only it could be true,
I'd share the dream with you too.
Perhaps it's in heaven where only goodness exists,
But my guess would be that even in heaven,
Change is on the list.

So, I'll think of it like the wind that I adore stroking my hair.
I'll embrace it like a hug and accept it like a dare.
I'll follow the turns and the kinks on my path,
I won't stop or turn or bother to look back.

Spirit Team, be with me I ask,
For dealing with change can be a hard task.

Daisy

Me in the making,
The creation of me.
Yet, selfless.
The gifts of trauma and trouble.
Peeling and unraveling the marks of time.
Sprouting growth.
The beauty of age as time allows;
Hugging the moments.
An empty body and plentiful mind.
Curiosity withstands,
A vessel traveling through space.
A heart thumping for joy and love,
The simple life.
A burning torch, flames of empathy;
Clear waters, known reality.
Judgment sleeps on a starry night,
And as the birds call the day to begin,
Peace settles in.
Triumphant through the darkness of doubt.
The yellow daisy blossoms, yellow.
So I, too
Bloom yellow.
Delicate yet bold;
Simply offering a smile.

A Space Inside Me

It's like a space inside me.
It's like the air I'm lucky to breathe.
It's an energy above my head.
It's the thoughts as I lie in my bed.
It's a hope for what I do not know.
It's a feeling sometimes I don't know how to show.
It's a calling from long ago.
It doesn't have a body but glides through space,
Sometimes I see it through the eyes on my face.
But mostly I feel, it's hard to explain.
I'm being drawn home, a one-way ticket on a plane.
Changes; indeed,
I'm not the same.
Spirit guides me; it's a whole new game.
Blessed and honored and led, I am.
Many blossoms since the journey began.
Yet more to come, to learn and grow,
Others to heal and love to sow.

Climbing Up

Climbing up to what rises inside
To be alone
To be without love in your home
A big space inside
Take me for a ride
Reach for rainbows, feel alive
Look at your life
Is there something you should do
What is it you know to be true

There are ants on the tree
Climbing up, what do they see
The sun smiles and the trees wave hello
Climbing up from the depths of darkness below
Peace, love, and joy
Think and it shall be
Feet resting on the trunk of a tree
This moment expands; shadows paint reality
Aches and pains subtly exist
Focusing on the moment, can't resist
Soak up the oranges and greens
Sitting here and jumping into dreams

LESS TEARS
NO FEARS

Being Alive Takes Time

Being alive takes time.
To feel each moment in space and time.
To have the courage to face the uncomfortable.
Tough situations with people you don't want to tackle.
To not worry about how they'll react,
To treat the incident as simply a fact.
Not a reflection of the love that you feel,
But a commitment to honesty and keeping it real.
To not take on the burden of others' pain,
And not let it influence you,
To stall or to refrain.
And if you find yourself in this struggle,
Is this an element of your shadow?
Often, we get bothered most
By our baggage, our junk,
And stories we wouldn't toast.
So when you seem to hesitate,
And you find yourself taken over by fear,
Pause for a moment
And look to see
If your shadow is near,
The grand reflection in the mirror.

The sky is always blue
blue & clear,
no clouds far or near
an upside down ocean
just lacking the motion.
different from one day
to the next.

Clear or cloudy,
The sun always sets.
Blue remains behind the storm,
Wait it out, for peace to return.
Free from the storm,
Rain washes away the past.
The sky opens,
New possibilities,
At last.
Grand blue, you knew,
As you looked down on me,
Small and fighting my enemies.
With a glance and a sigh,
Thoughts changed under the blue, blue sky.
Steadily blue,
Behind the red sunset too.
The balance of the hue.
Mother Nature painted you up high.
Love and protection from the blue, blue sky.

The Treasure Inside

The treasure inside.
What makes you feel alive,
Who holds the key,
To all you want to be.
Locked up for eternity,
Lost for no one to see.

The gift unwrapped,
Scared and trapped.
Tear it apart,
Shine the light on the dark.

There's a story to be told,
Knowledge to unfold.
Sound the starting bell,
Paint, rhythms, and rhymes do tell.
Shake the unworthy spell.
Cast about, let creativity shout.

Sad is the unlived life,
Suppressed with the treasure still inside.
Squat upon sameness, let your truth fly.
Like a colorful meadow,
Spring flowers reaching for the sky.

Your gifts are meant to be seen, to be shared.
The treasure you possess, treat it with care.
Rip the wrapping away,
From your truth do not stray.

Curiosity Cove

In the mysterious woods of Curiosity Cove,
Read the sign -
You're Welcome Here from Wherever You Drove.
Red hair, black skin, tattoos, and next to kin.
Loud and soft, those that sleep, those that rock.
Bring a candle and a guitar too.
Shoes are optional, there ain't many rules.
You have to be you, no need to be cool.
Your shoulders drop,
Your pulse begins to slow.
The green is greener, your aura begins to grow.
Red, purple, and yellow,
Sitting on a stump with a wise fellow.
Squirrels and rabbits scurry about, pure radiance, no doubt.
In Curiosity Cove, mystery unfolds, water trickles about.
Harmony greets its name, nothing is the same, all beauty,
It's so insane.
It's real, it's not a game.
Walking through the meadow, feet taking no blame.
You are you, there is no shame.
Authentic and pure, perfection stakes its claim.

What if leprechauns were real
The green, the jolly
A pot of gold to steal.

What if miracles were true,
Possible for me and possible for you.
No doubt, faith,
No figuring it out.

What if war didn't exist,
No fighting, no guns
Only hugs and kisses.
What if nobody cared about the clothes you wear,
Or the color of your hair.

What if people didn't judge,
And only showed love.

What if nobody bragged,
Nobody was left out.
All for one and one for all,
Peaceful encounters, no violent brawls.

What if you could see my soul,
If your eyes had special vision,
And you were brave and bold.
No fear of the future,
Or focus on the past,
Present each day as if it were your last.

What if there was only one mood,

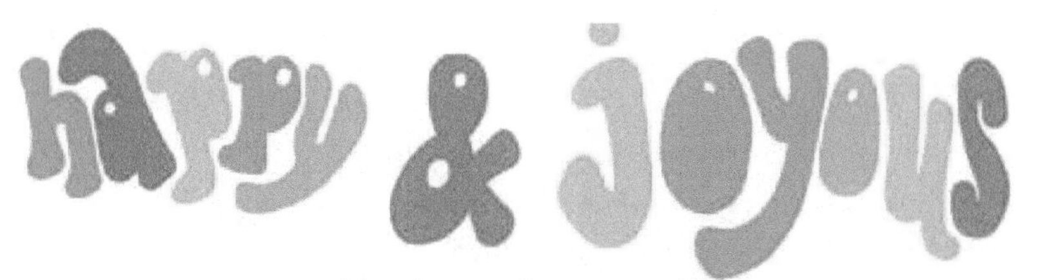

No depression or anxiety,
No pressure from society.

What if you were free to dream,
Felt free to scream,
Felt true to yourself,
Not be part of the scene.
What if life was really magical,
Fall down,

And grow a new tentacle.
The road isn't smooth for most and many,
But blessings and insights,
Exist and there's plenty.

Focus on gratitude and all that you have.
Keep the vibration of joy in your head.
The universe will respond,

You might find a pot of gold
To sit upon.

All I Have Is Me

All I have is me.
I start with me; I end with me.
And in between, there might be you, but really there is just me.
I'm the one who's in charge of my mind.
I'm the one who decides to be kind.
It's me who sets me free,
It's me who decides how to be.
Oh, yes, there's you, and I like that too,
But, you could leave me, and forsake me.
And then it's just me again.
Just as I began.
You see,
There's really just me.
And yes, there's them, and their fun now and then.
But they have their ways, their interests, and their days.
And then, I'm stuck with me, you see.
So here I am,
Feeling all of me,
It's warm and secure,
But a little lonely.
It's not new to me, but how could it be?
It's not that I don't want to be alone,
In fact it feels very much like home.
But what I feel is like the ocean so deep,
There's a lot of water under my feet.
Below the surface lives passion and fire,
Thoughts and emotions of dreams and desires.
It's seems like a lot, and I don't always let it out,
So all this rumbling just spins about.
I keep it for me, sometimes sharing with the trees.
If you all knew all this crazy in me,
You may just stay away, carried away by the cool breeze.
So as much as I share,
There's so much more I don't dare.
As the sun goes down, painting the sky of my cute little town,

I feel the connection all around.
Yet, there's times when I know
That really there's just me.
It's me who chooses how I approach each day.
What I focus on, what I want to play.
It's me who suffers from the choices I make,
It's me who grips the guilt for no one to take.
I am the one who decides to have fun, to lie in the sun,
To take a beach run.
True, there's my friends, and I enjoy each one.
Without them my life would be less fun,
Adventures I would not have done.
But still, it's me, my head feels heavy.
My mind is split between the clouds and my heart.
It's I who must figure it all out,
It is I who is aware of these feeling as sharp as a dart.
It's just me, you see.
I'm stuck with me to please.
That's not such a bad thing I see.
I am authentic, secure, and free.
I can control how I'd like to be.
I can share what I like and choose to have no fright.
Just me doesn't have to feel lonely.
I want to be authentically me, such a powerful plea.
A statement all may strive to be.
So even at my best, when it comes time to rest,
When it's quiet or I'm sad, I know that I'm all I have.
So I may as well get comfortable in my own skin,
There's really no better way to win.
I was born a perfect creation from my mom and my dad.
Love and joy, so much I have had.
So even if I feel misunderstood,
If my passions are hiding under the hood,
If I feel frustrated, desperate, or lonely,
I can close my eyes and throw away sad, grabbing onto glad.
For even if it is just me, I know who I am,
And...that's just enough.

Loving Life

Wanting it all and more than that.
Loving life and funky hats.
Seeing the world and sharing a laugh.
Sitting in the sand with a pen in hand.
Creativity and expression, ideas, and inventions.
Plump with passion,
Make it all happen.
Slow the moments, give me more time.
So much to do, to be, and to find.
A magical garden,
Fruit on every vine,
Colors so bright,
Visible to even the blind.
Music plays,
And dancing breaks out.
People are in love,
And there is no doubt.
The world swirls in the colorful rainbow above,
Sharing and giving,
So much love.

BE

Be in the present moment.
Seems like I've written this before,
Yet as the day turns to night,
And I continue to write, it sinks into my skin,
And I begin to understand,
Nothing external can be sustained.
I feel the joy in releasing the pain of the grip.
I clench so tight, searching for delight,
Dreaming of what might be,
And yet,
It already is.
So I sit, as the water before me ripples,
And the whispers of the wind blow,
And I go within to absorb the Isness again.
Fifty-six years it's been, for me to understand
My mind will set me free.
Grace, drip your golden glow upon my head,
Let it flow down my limbs as I begin,
To be right here,
Right now,
Again.
Let my energy rise, let me be wise,
And BE with all that is before my eyes.

About the Illustrator

Brooke Kelley is a freelance artist living in Kauai where she surfs, skates, gardens, paints and sews. Her love for life flows through the colors and shapes, and her child-like nature unfolds with each work of art. The way she interprets life through images mixes magically with the way Jen weaves her words.

"Jen's poetry has had a profound and peaceful effect on me. I was so excited to work with her and portray my art to create a book that I know will make people feel free and inspired. It was in working with Jen as a life coach and creating a friendship that I began to feel empowered and free to follow my dream. I hope this book makes you feel the same too."

To follow Brooke or purchase her creations go to:
IG:@bevyandbrine
etsy.com/shop/bevyandbrine

About the Author

Jen Adams lives by the beach in Southern California and is the mom of two young renaissance men ages, 20 and 22. She's an outdoor enthusiast and loves traveling in her renovated Dodge ProMaster van named Daisy, her mobile office. She can be found walking on the beach, playing on the sand volleyball court near her house, in the mountains with a pack next to a stream, or at a table with friends and family, accompanied by good music, games, dancing and great food. Jen's laugh and joy for life is contagious. Vitamin is her joy, laughter her medicine, nature her god. Her lifelong journey is to understand the subtle nuances of life, to find meaning in the unseen, and to translate her perceptions through rhyme. She invites the reader to an experience that leaves them filling full of light. Writing is the common thread that weaves the life of Jen's many passions.
She is a National Board-Certified Health and Wellness Coach, a Mindset Coach, a Mindfulness Teacher, an Energy Healer, and Poet. Her passion is to inspire people to see their inner beauty and live their lives to the fullest.

To follow Jen:
IG:@sagesoulandflowers
www.jenadamscoaching.com
zenjenadams@gmail.com

Made in the USA
Columbia, SC
07 November 2021